SCIENCE KIDS

The Changing Earth

HOW WATER SHAPES THE EARTH

Jared Siemens

www.av2books.com

LET'S READ
AV²
BY WEIGL™
ADDED VALUE • AUDIO VISUAL

Go to **www.av2books.com**, and enter this book's unique code.

BOOK CODE

X8549

AV² by Weigl brings you media enhanced books that support active learning.

AV² provides enriched content that supplements and complements this book. Weigl's AV² books strive to create inspired learning and engage young minds in a total learning experience.

Your AV² Media Enhanced books come alive with...

Audio
Listen to sections of the book read aloud.

Video
Watch informative video clips.

Embedded Weblinks
Gain additional information for research.

Try This!
Complete activities and hands-on experiments.

Key Words
Study vocabulary, and complete a matching word activity.

Quizzes
Test your knowledge.

Slide Show
View images and captions, and prepare a presentation.

... and much, much more!

Published by AV² by Weigl
350 5th Avenue, 59th Floor   New York, NY   10118
Websites: www.av2books.com   www.weigl.com

Library of Congress Control Number: 2014942103

ISBN 978-1-4896-1926-6 (hardcover)
ISBN 978-1-4896-1927-3 (softcover)
ISBN 978-1-4896-1928-0 (single user eBook)
ISBN 978-1-4896-1929-7 (multi-user eBook)

Printed in the United States of America in North Mankato, Minnesota
1 2 3 4 5 6 7 8 9 0   18 17 16 15 14

062014
WEP030614

Every reasonable effort has been made to trace ownership and to obtain permission to reprint copyright material. The publishers would be pleased to have any errors or omissions brought to their attention so that they may be corrected in subsequent printings.

Weigl acknowledges Getty Images as the primary image supplier for this title.

Project Coordinator: Jared Siemens
Designer: Mandy Christiansen

CONTENTS

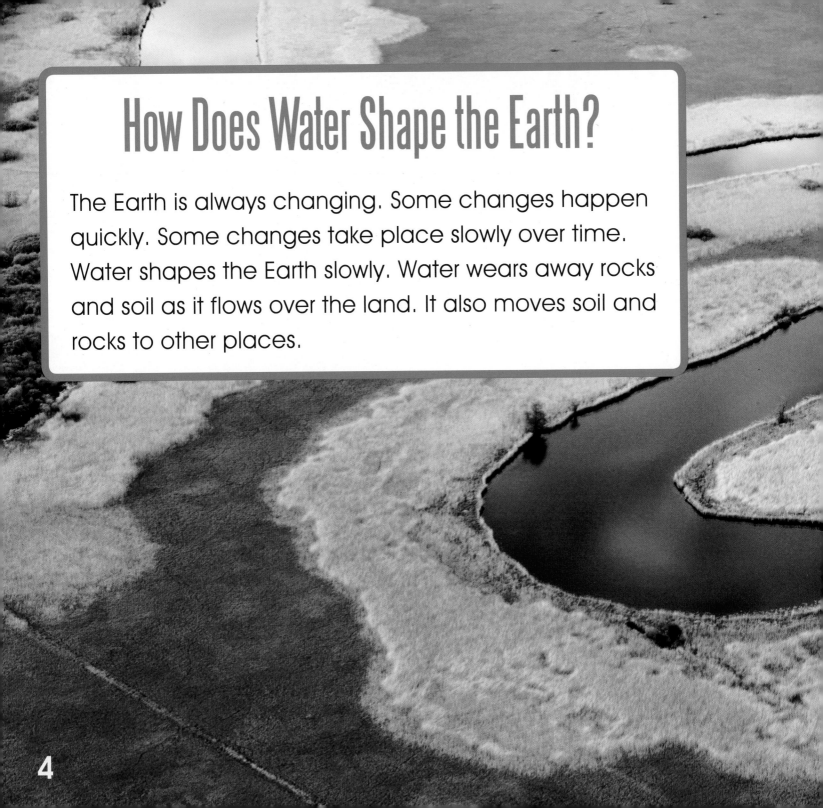

How Does Water Shape the Earth?

The Earth is always changing. Some changes happen quickly. Some changes take place slowly over time. Water shapes the Earth slowly. Water wears away rocks and soil as it flows over the land. It also moves soil and rocks to other places.

5

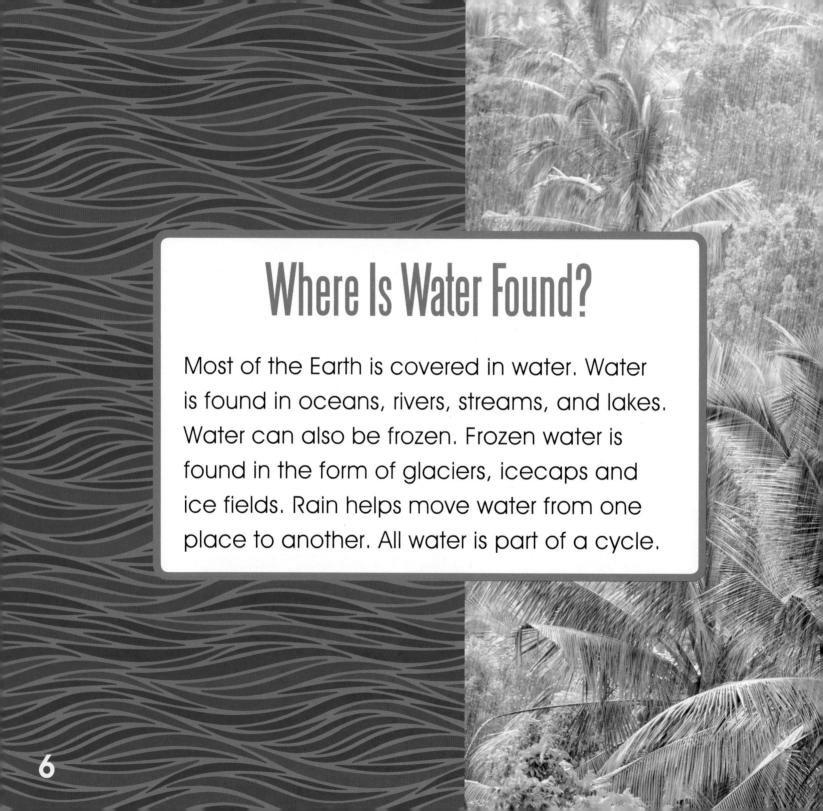

Where Is Water Found?

Most of the Earth is covered in water. Water is found in oceans, rivers, streams, and lakes. Water can also be frozen. Frozen water is found in the form of glaciers, icecaps and ice fields. Rain helps move water from one place to another. All water is part of a cycle.

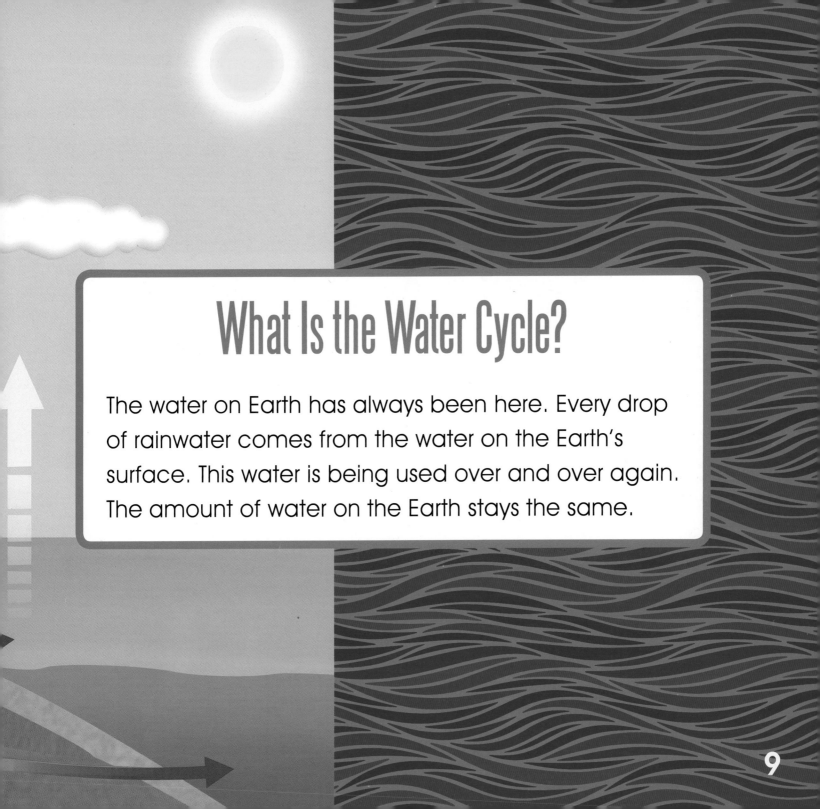

What Is the Water Cycle?

The water on Earth has always been here. Every drop of rainwater comes from the water on the Earth's surface. This water is being used over and over again. The amount of water on the Earth stays the same.

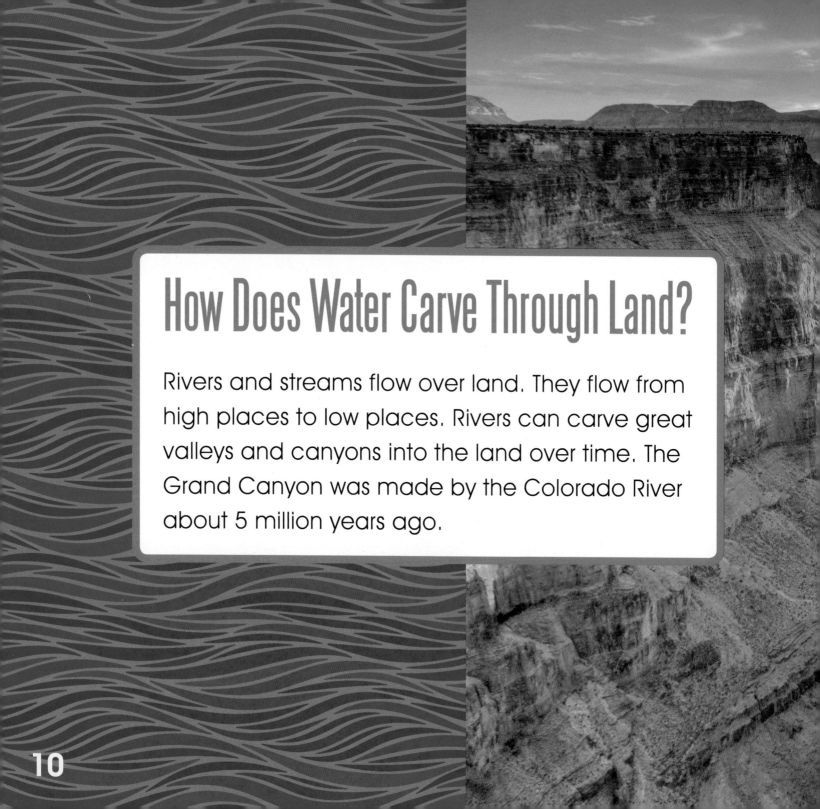

How Does Water Carve Through Land?

Rivers and streams flow over land. They flow from high places to low places. Rivers can carve great valleys and canyons into the land over time. The Grand Canyon was made by the Colorado River about 5 million years ago.

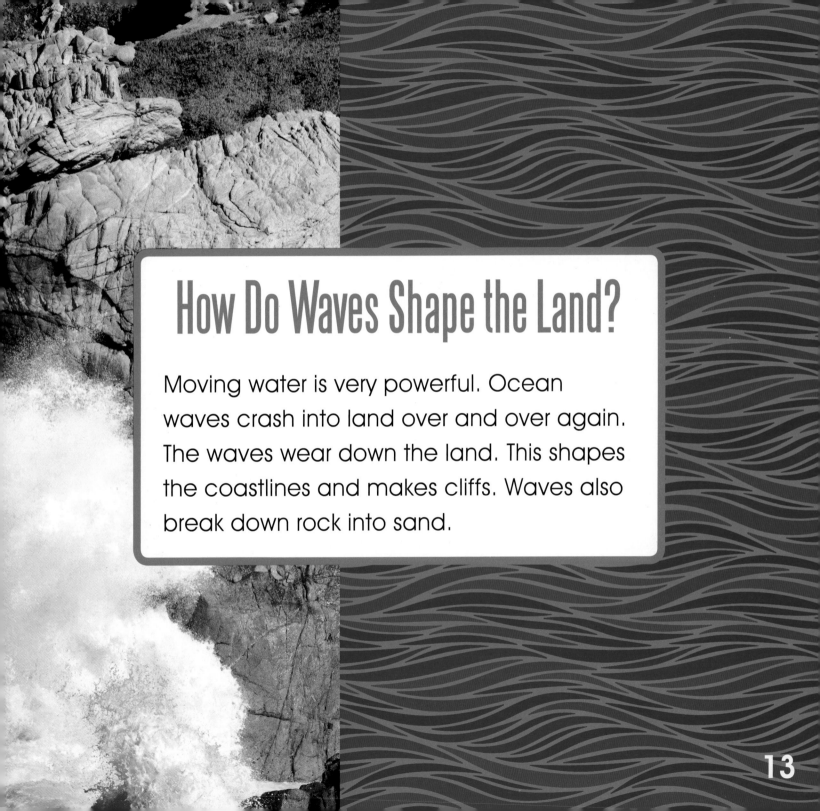

How Do Waves Shape the Land?

Moving water is very powerful. Ocean waves crash into land over and over again. The waves wear down the land. This shapes the coastlines and makes cliffs. Waves also break down rock into sand.

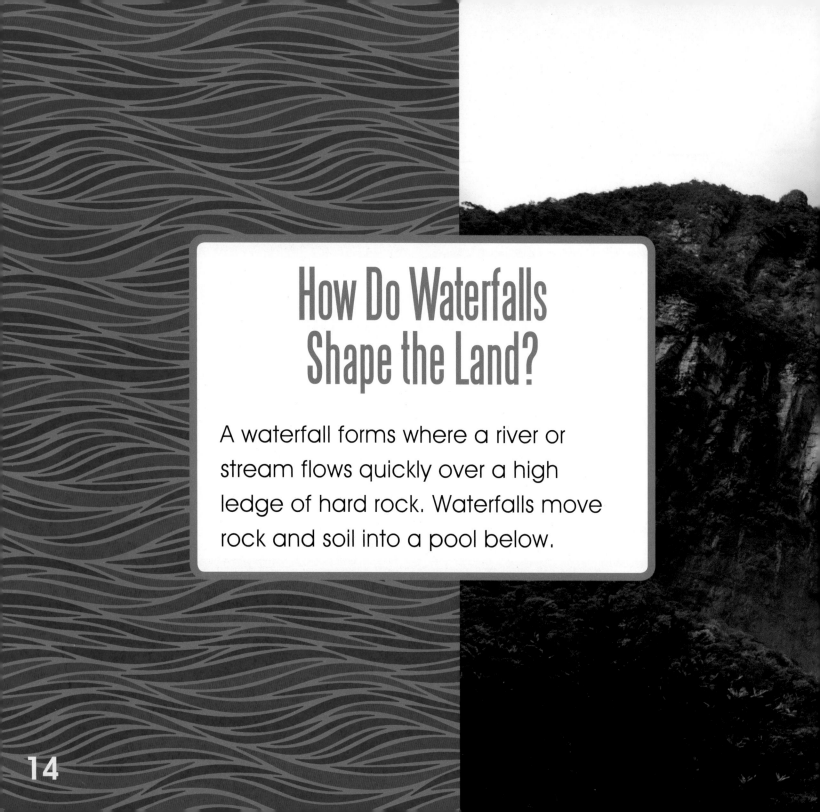

How Do Waterfalls Shape the Land?

A waterfall forms where a river or stream flows quickly over a high ledge of hard rock. Waterfalls move rock and soil into a pool below.

How Do Glaciers Shape the Land?

Glaciers are large pieces of frozen water that move slowly over the land. They drag pieces of rock and soil along with them as they move. Sometimes when glaciers melt they leave large rocks behind. Some rocks break apart when water freezes in their cracks. This can change the shape of mountains and the land around them.

How Does Water Destroy the Land?

Water changes the land quickly during natural disasters such as floods, hurricanes, and tsunamis. Floods destroy farmland by washing away the topsoil that helps plants grow. Hurricanes and tsunamis can ruin coastal cities and wash away the homes of people living there.

19

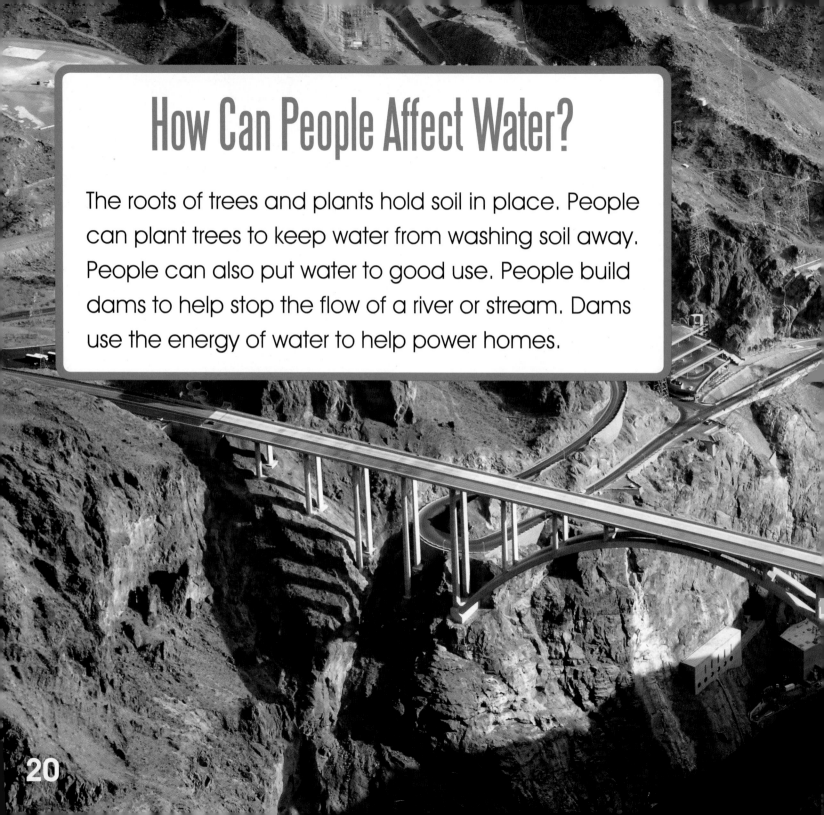

How Can People Affect Water?

The roots of trees and plants hold soil in place. People can plant trees to keep water from washing soil away. People can also put water to good use. People build dams to help stop the flow of a river or stream. Dams use the energy of water to help power homes.

WATER FACTS

These pages provide detailed information that expands on the interesting facts found in the book. These pages are intended to be used by adults to help young readers round out their knowledge of each of the natural forces featured in the *Science Kids: The Changing Earth* series.

Pages 4–5

How Does Water Shape the Earth? The surface of Earth is constantly changing. Land is changed by forces on the surface and deep underground. Water is one of the most powerful forces on the planet. It is one of the main causes of weathering and erosion. Weathering is a process of rock wearing away from the land, while erosion carries these worn away pieces to new places. Rainfall, rivers, and ocean waves all contribute to weathering and erosion, which transforms coastlines, mountains, and other landforms over time.

Pages 6–7

Where Is Water Found? Approximately 70 percent of the Earth's surface is covered in water. The saltwater in the oceans makes up about 97 percent of the Earth's water. Glaciers and icecaps account for another 2 percent. The remaining 1 percent of water on Earth is freshwater stored underground and as surface water such as lakes, rivers, and streams.

Pages 8–9

What Is the Water Cycle? The water cycle is the process of water changing forms and moving from one place to another. Water changes from a liquid to a gas when the Sun heats the surface of a body of water. This gas, called water vapor, rises upwards with warm air. When the water vapor reaches cooler air, or the amount of vapor becomes too heavy for the air to hold, it condenses back into a liquid or solid. The water falls back to the ground in the form of rain or snow. This precipitation helps replenish lakes, rivers, and groundwater.

Pages 10–11

How Does Water Carve Through Land? Rivers pick up soil, pebbles, and rocks from along the river bottom and carry them further downstream. This material is called sediment. As a river flows, sediment wears down the banks and bed of the river, changing its shape. The faster a river is, the more sediment it can carry. Rivers eventually deposit sediment in new places. Large pieces of sediment are left behind as the river slows down, until only the smallest particles are left in the water. Sediment usually gathers on river banks, deltas, and at the bottom of waterfalls.

How Do Waves Shape the Land? Coastal erosion is caused by physical and chemical forces weathering and eroding the rock. As waves pound the shore, rock and sand in the water have a sandpaper effect on the faces of cliffs. Some ocean water contains acids that can break down rocks such as limestone and chalk. Over time, these processes create cliffs, caves, and sea stacks. The coast continues to move slowly inland as the waves carry away pieces of the shore.

How Do Waterfalls Shape the Land? Waterfalls form as water flows over and erodes soft rock, leaving a precipice of hard rock. Waterfalls are divided into two types, either cataracts or cascades. A cataract is a tall waterfall with a large volume of water flowing over its precipice. Angel Falls in Venezuela is the world's highest cataract. A small stream of the Churún River falls 3,212 feet (979 meters) down the face of a cliff. Cascades occur when a river slopes downward slightly to a lower level, causing the water to leap gently from rock to rock.

How Do Glaciers Shape the Land? The term glacier comes from the French word *glace*, meaning "ice". Gravity pulls the heavy ice down mountainsides and valleys. Each part of the glacier moves at different speeds. This creates tension in the glacier, causing the upper ice to fracture. Most glaciers move less than 2 inches per day (3-4 centimeters). Fast-moving rivers of ice, called galloping glaciers, travel up to 160 feet (50 meters) a day.

How Does Water Destroy the Land? Hurricanes are circulating storms that form over warm areas of the ocean. Hurricanes bring intense rains, high waves, and extreme winds that exceed 150 miles (240 kilometers) per hour. Tsunamis are giant ocean waves often caused by earthquakes or volcanic eruptions. One of the deadliest tsunamis in history originated near Sumatra, Indonesia in December 2004. The tsunami killed more than 200,000 people.

How Can People Affect Water? Planting trees and other vegetation can protect soil from the eroding effects of overland flooding. However, not all floods are bad for soil. Floodwaters can deposit nutrients, minerals, and other organic materials in the soil that are beneficial to crop growth. Prior to the construction of the Aswan High Dam, the Nile River in Egypt flooded the nearby plains each spring. Egyptian people relied on this annual flood to enrich the soil and water their crops.

KEY WORDS

Research has shown that as much as 65 percent of all written material published in English is made up of 300 words. These 300 words cannot be taught using pictures or learned by sounding them out. They must be recognized by sight. This book contains 88 common sight words to help young readers improve their reading fluency and comprehension. This book also teaches young readers several important content words, such as nouns. These words are paired with pictures to aid in learning and improve understanding.

Page	Sight Words First Appearance
4	also, always, and, as, away, changes, does, earth, how, is, it, land, moves, other, over, place, some, take, the, time, to, water
6	a, all, another, be, can, found, helps, in, most, of, one, part, rivers, where
9	again, been, being, comes, every, has, here, on, same, this, used, what
10	about, by, great, high, into, made, they, through, was, years
13	do, down, makes, very
14	below, hard, or
17	along, are, around, large, leave, mountains, sometimes, that, their, them, when, with
18	grow, homes, people, plants, such, there
20	good, keep, put, stop, trees

Page	Content Words First Appearance
4	rocks, soil
6	cycle, form, glaciers, icecaps, ice fields, lakes, oceans, rain, streams
9	amount, drop, rainwater, surface
10	canyons, Colorado River, Grand Canyon, million, valleys
13	cliffs, coastlines, sand, waves
14	ledge, pool, waterfalls
17	cracks, pieces, shape
18	cities, farmland, floods, hurricanes, natural disasters, topsoil, tsunamis
20	dams, energy, flow, power, roots

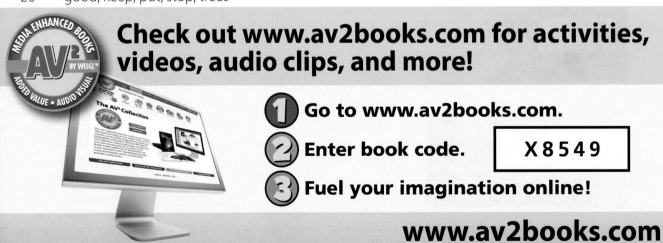

Check out www.av2books.com for activities, videos, audio clips, and more!

1 Go to www.av2books.com.

2 Enter book code. X 8 5 4 9

3 Fuel your imagination online!

www.av2books.com